You've Got Manners!
Youthful Dining Etiquette

Table Tips from A to Z
for Kids of All Ages

by Louise Elerding

You've Got Manners!
Youthful Dining Etiquette

Table Tips from A to Z
for Kids of All Ages
Second Edition

Written and Illustrated by Louise Elerding
Layout and Color Design by Bruce Gordon

Grandy Publications
Burbank, California

ISBN-13: 978-0-9729237-0-5
ISBN-10: 0-9729237-0-5
Library of Congress Control Number: 2003104959

Other books written by Louise Elerding:
¡Ya tienes buenos modales! (You've Got Manners!–Spanish Edition)
You've Got Manners! (portable handbook)
Formulas For Dressing The Whole Person
You've Got Social Manners!

To order additional copies of books, call 800-326-8953 or email MannersA2Z@aol.com
Visit us at www.youvegotmanners.com

Printed in China

Dedication

To my 5 sensational grandkids – who are an invaluable Advisory Board.
In 'A to Z' order, with love to Alyssa, Amanda, Emily, Jason and Tyler. Their clever ideas, observations, refreshing perspectives, and delightful sense of humor, became a book.

Acknowledgments to:
(In 'A to Z' order)

Angie – my 'angel-ita', whose love, coaching, & encouragement of 'boundaryless creativity' inspires me always;

Brenda – the bright beacon of immeasurable support and infinite Sissy-B friendship;

Cindy – for our hours of entrepreneurship talk-a-thons and vigorous laughter ;

Evana – my Star Buddy, who intuitively put a pen in my hand several years ago;

Grancy – my spiritual mentor who knows that love is all there is;

GoGo's: Lani, Mags and Pam – the best breakfast-bunch of issue-dishing girlfriends ever;

Joyce – who shares in every 'goosebump' as we tread new waters beside each other;

Karenlee – whose perpetual loving nudges always keep me growing;

McMabble Sisters, whose hearts, ears, & minds are always there with a cheering safety net;

Michael – whose solid guidance and sturdy hand, always included space for the big vision;

Nannette – a genuine talent who sincerely supports our friendship and artsy adventures;

Olivia – my beautiful soul-sister who always makes time to listen and care;

Renee – a soul-pal whose light & love were keys for opening bigger doors;

Susie – the consummate pro-active cheer-leader and very best lovefriend;

Wes, Alyson, Tom, Augie, & Kristin, – my remarkable family who cheerfully participated in this project every 'letter' of the way.

TABLE TIPS
from A to Z

man.ners (man / ers), n. ways of behaving with
reference to polite standards: good manners.

What makes a good manner ? What if you can't find the answer in any etiquette book ?

You will always be able to show good manners at any time if you just ask yourself this question:
"Is what I am doing considerate of the other people and circumstances around me ? "

As you read each of these TIPS see if you can tell in what way they are being
thoughtful or helpful to others.

Whether you are at home or in public, good manners are easy and fun — and make parents very proud.
Best of all, the person displaying good manners feels good about the way they are acting,
and it's catchy — so it inspires others to do the same.

With all of us working together as the Polite Team, the world is going to be filled with
well-mannered, kindly people.

Remember to keep it happy !

Dear _____

(This book belongs to you.)

Hi!

We are Polly Politely
and Milton Manners,
here to take you on
a table manners adventure.

Bring us to the table with you,
or put us on your
night stand, or bring us
along for a ride in your car.

When you look at us –
remember what fun it is
to have good table manners.

We'll be watching out for you!

And look in the back of the book for
your "certificate" – showing that
you've learned your manners well.

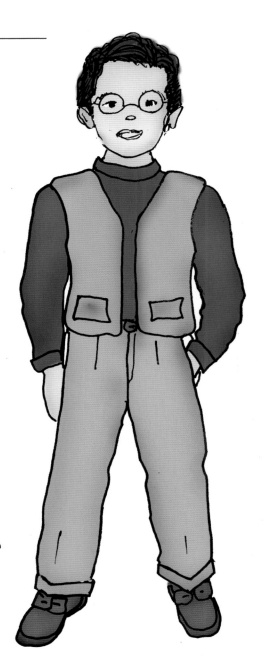

Fork   Knife Spoon

Alphabetically! Your "fork – knife – spoon" placement around your plate
is in alphabetical order!

At your place-setting, you will find your napkin laying to the left of your fork.

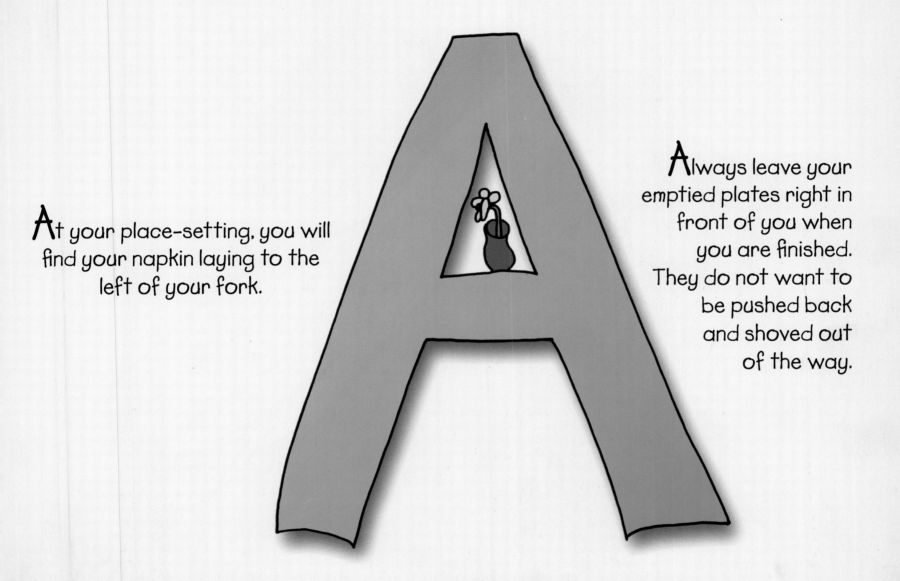

Always leave your emptied plates right in front of you when you are finished. They do not want to be pushed back and shoved out of the way.

Before eating or drinking, remove your gloves.

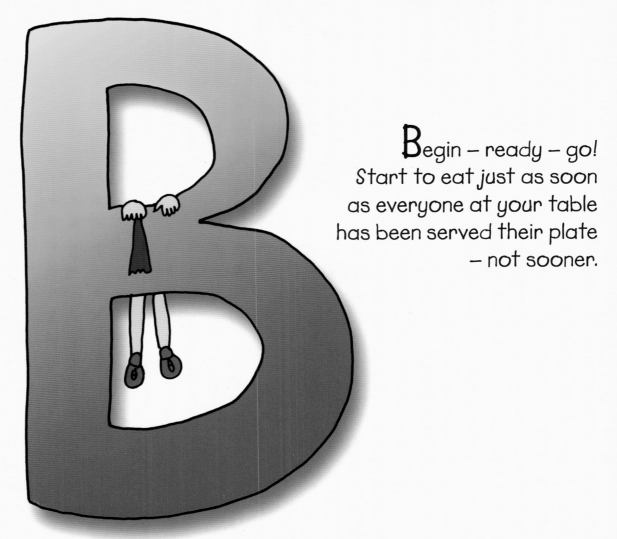

Begin – ready – go!
Start to eat just as soon
as everyone at your table
has been served their plate
– not sooner.

Blowing your nose at the table is like "hide & seek."
Seek a Kleenex and hide your face away from the people sitting with you.
Just turn your head away, or look down, while blowing.

Check to see where each piece of your place setting is: (1) your main plate in front of you, (2) bread plate above your fork, (3) salad plate to the left of fork. Utensils: (4) salad fork & (5) dinner fork on left side of plate, (6) beverage glass above knife, (7) knife, (8) teaspoon, and (9) soup spoon on the right of the main plate.

Count the donuts – or anything else you are offered – to be sure there is enough for everyone at the table. If there are 8 donuts on the tray, and 8 people at the table, that means you take just one.

Combing hair around food could be hazardous to what lands on your plate. Never groom at the table.

Dessert utensils get "TOP PRIORITY" when added to the basic place-setting. They will be found "at the top" – above the plate.

Don't reach across someone – always ask for items to be passed.

Dropping a utensil or food on the floor happens. Leave it there, and the waiter will pick it up later. Meanwhile, ask for a replacement utensil.

"Excuse me!" Some countries consider burping a compliment, but NOT in the USA. No burping please. If you do this by accident, a quiet "excuse me" is polite – and quickly move on to talk about something else.

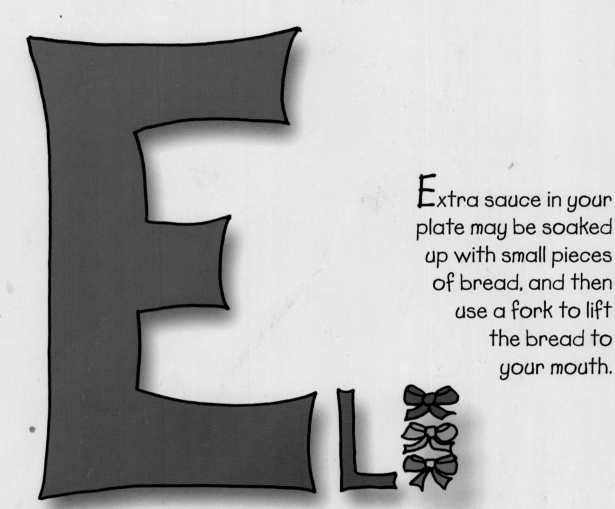

Elbows are placed "downtown," off the table, with your spare hand on your lap, and the "worker" hand at the table.

Extra sauce in your plate may be soaked up with small pieces of bread, and then use a fork to lift the bread to your mouth.

Finished? The signal that you are finished eating is to place your fork and knife at 3:50 o'clock. This tells the waiter to clear your plate.

Finger bowls are sometimes given to you at the end of a meal or at the end of a course. Dip your fingers into the water quickly (like a cat who hates water, skipping through a rain puddle). Then wipe your hands on your napkin, below the table.

Finger foods, like an airplane, need to land somewhere first. Put finger foods on a plate, or on a napkin FIRST... THEN put into your mouth. No direct flights from the serving dish into the mouth.

17

Gum takes a detour. Instead of going with you to the dinner table, it heads for a rest-stop in the waste basket. It *NEVER* wants to be squished or stuck underneath the table top.

Is there a special Guest or an adult at your table that you can pull a chair out for? This deserves extra credit !

Get the waiter's attention with a gentle hand signal, soft voice and eye contact – waiting until that person is within a few feet of you.

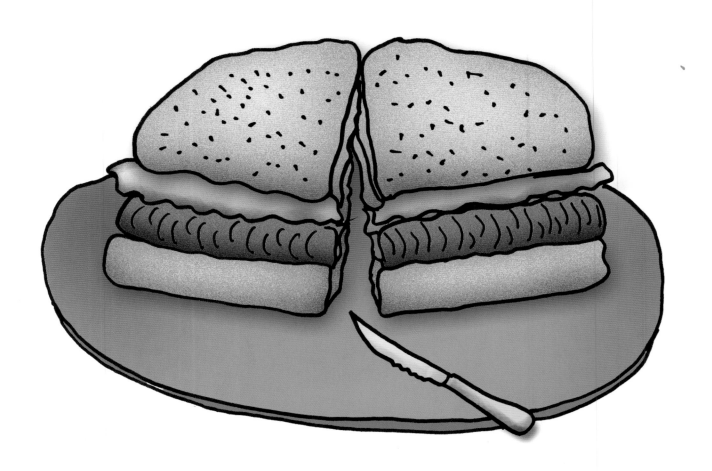

Hamburgers and other big sandwiches need cutting.
Slice them in half, using your knife.

Hats off to gentlemen! No hats or hoods at the table for boys. Girls, you get to keep them on.

Hang your coat over the back of your chair, unless you want to check it in the cloak room. It's way too crowded to fit all of that on your lap ... you need room for your napkin!

21

Hi! This is my friend Amanda—the girl I told you would be here today.

Hi! What's your name?

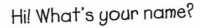

Hello, my name is Tyler. What's yours?

Goodbye! It was fun getting to know you!

See you later— let's call each other tomorrow.

Bye Alyssa! I hope we get to see each other again soon.

Introduce each other at your table, and ask everyone's name.
Say "goodbye" to everyone when you leave.

Ice stays in your glass
– it doesn't go into
your mouth like chewing
gum. No chewing ice
at the table.

Important people,
and a guest of honor,
always sit to the right
of the host.

23

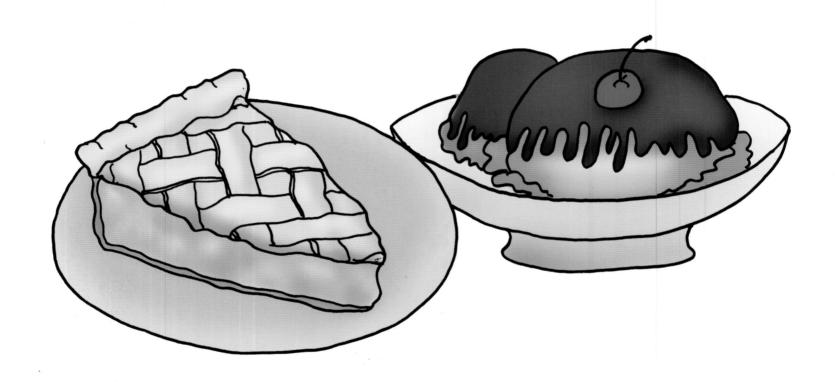

Just like waiting for everyone to be served before you start to eat your meal...
also wait for everyone to receive their dessert before you begin eating that too.

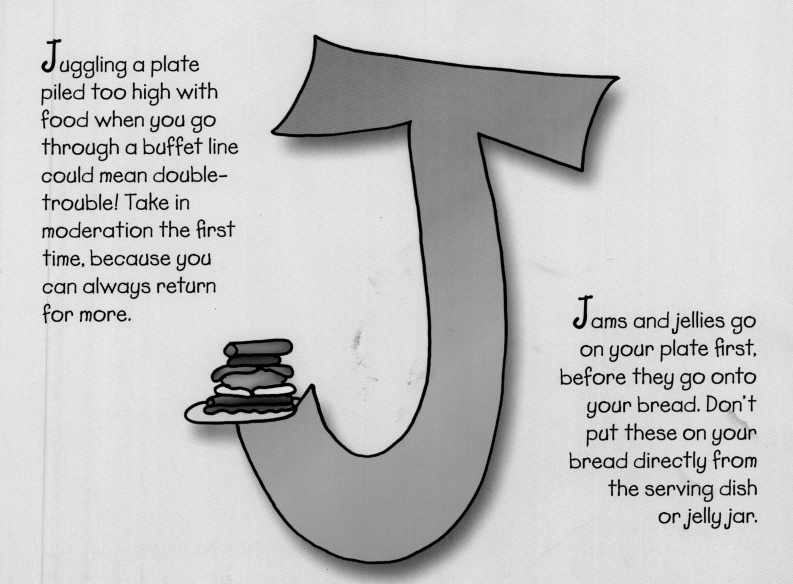

Juggling a plate piled too high with food when you go through a buffet line could mean double-trouble! Take in moderation the first time, because you can always return for more.

Jams and jellies go on your plate first, before they go onto your bread. Don't put these on your bread directly from the serving dish or jelly jar.

25

Knives go to New Hampshire...rest it on the upper right corner
– northeast side – of your dinner plate.

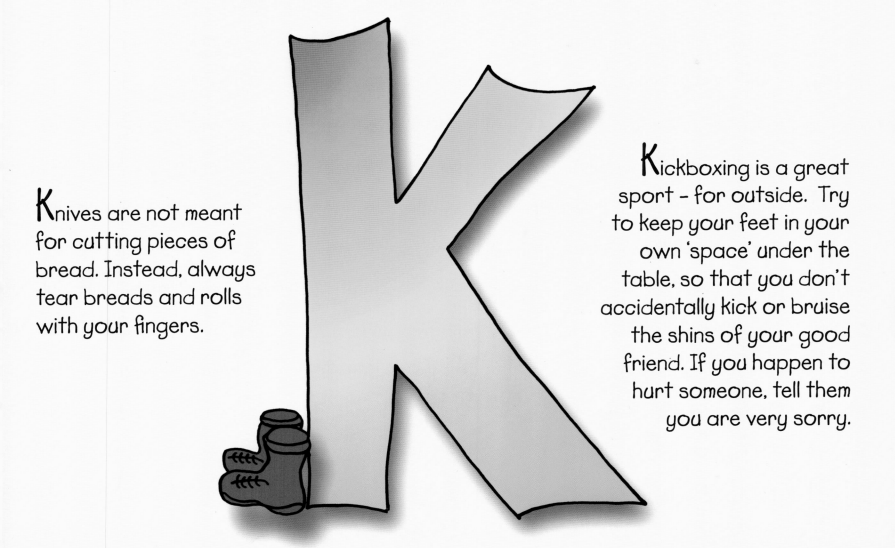

Knives are not meant for cutting pieces of bread. Instead, always tear breads and rolls with your fingers.

Kickboxing is a great sport – for outside. Try to keep your feet in your own 'space' under the table, so that you don't accidentally kick or bruise the shins of your good friend. If you happen to hurt someone, tell them you are very sorry.

"Left side entrance and exit" ... enter and leave your chair from the left side.

Look at your host
and FOLLOW –THE–
LEADER, whenever
you are not sure of
which utensil to use,
what to do, or how
to eat something
new and different.
Just do it the way
they do.

Lipstick
application is an art,
so take your tools
to the powder room
– "paint" there, not
at the table.

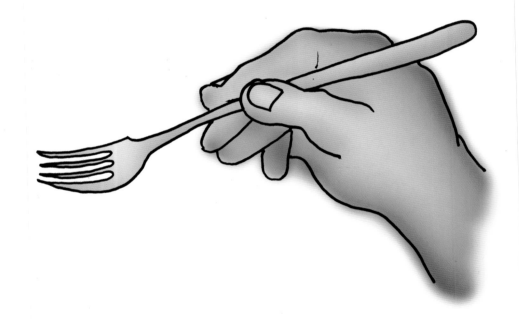

Most of the time you will want to hold your fork like a pencil – never overhand like a garden shovel or a pitch fork.

Make friendly table conversation: ask questions about others, share news, and tell fun stories.

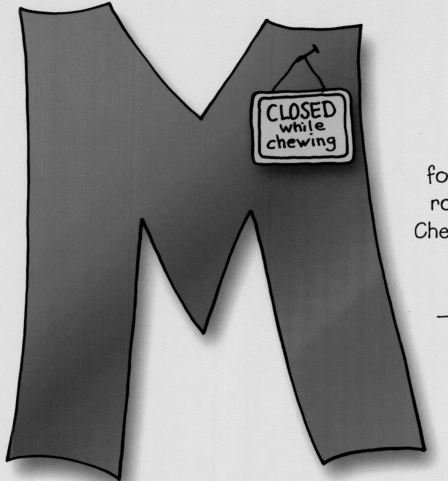

CLOSED while chewing

Mouth full of food ... leaves no room for talking. Chew well – mouth "CLOSED" for the time being – swallow, THEN speak.

Napkins get to sit on your chair and wait for you there
(not on the table) if you need to leave for a moment during the meal.

Napkins go on your lap right away — just as soon as you sit down on your chair.

Neatly place your napkin back on the table when you are finally finished with your meal, and ready to go.
(It started on the table, and it ends on the table.)

Once in awhile, check to see if you need to wipe your mouth or face while eating.
Yes, good choice...you're using your napkin – not your sleeve!
A clean face means no disgrace.

Only cut one bite of food at a time – then eat that piece. If you're not of age to use a knife yet, then it's OK to have Mom or Dad cut you several bites ahead of time.

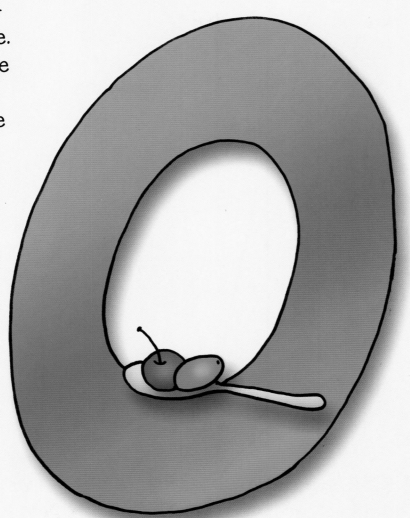

Olive pits, cherry pits or anything that surprises you and you don't want in your mouth, gets carried out of your mouth by a fork or spoon, and quietly put on the edge of your plate. No comment about it, pleeze !

Pepper & Salt are best friends and always travel together. Even when only one is asked to go somewhere, they both go. Always pass them together. Hold them by their sides (not over their shakers).

Purses don't eat – so they prefer to sit on your lap or hang from the back of your chair, or be put on the floor – never on the table.

Pieces of food that get caught in your braces will act like a pest until you fix it. Excuse yourself from the table and do this in private in the rest room.

Quickly put your spoon on the saucer when finished with your soup –
don't leave it standing there, all alone and lonesome, in the bowl.

Quietly scoop your
soup with a gentle
loop: dip spoon
away from you
toward the rear
of the bowl.

Questions asked
to you while you are
eating something,
can wait to be
answered until you
have swallowed all
of your food. Then
speak right up.

"Right on" is right ... means everything gets passed on to the right. This avoids traffic congestion on the food highway... always take the RIGHT-of-way.

Rest your cutting knife on the plate edge while you chew. Give it a time out. You don't need to keep holding it in your hand in-between cuttings.

Rocking chairs have rounded rocker-legs. Dining chairs have straight legs. So that's the clue to keep all four straight-legs flat on the floor. No "rocking out" or tipping back your chair during meals.

Sugar and cream are passed and then placed on the table in front of the person who asked for them – with handles turned toward that person.

*S*traws stay in the glass at all times. They never blow bubbles, or make 'empty-glass' tunes.

*S*paghetti and other long pasta "hasta" be cut, or rolled in a spoon. No pretending they are tall sucking-straws.

Tear off one bite-size piece of bread at a time, and butter only that one piece — then eat it. When you are ready for another taste of bread, tear another bite-size piece off, and just butter that piece. We never butter the whole slice of bread, or the whole roll, all at once.

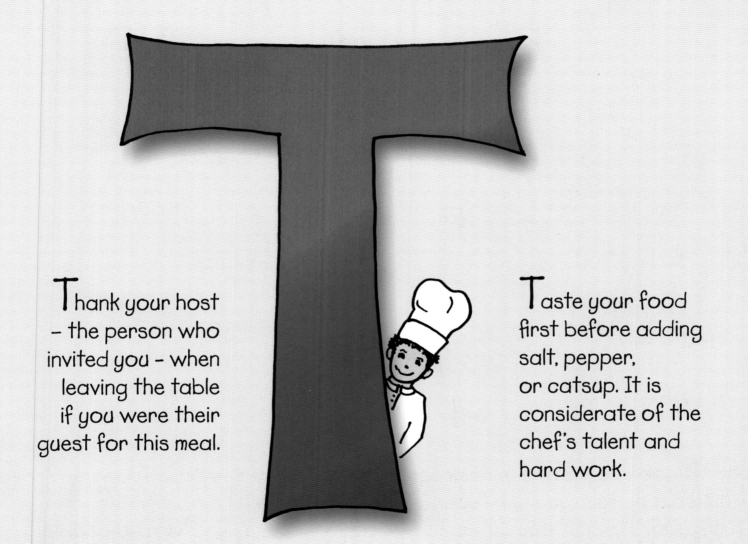

Thank your host – the person who invited you – when leaving the table if you were their guest for this meal.

Taste your food first before adding salt, pepper, or catsup. It is considerate of the chef's talent and hard work.

Unless the whole room is doing a song – there's no singing at the table.
If you're at home and dying to sing...teach everyone else your song too.

Use your very own place-setting butter knife when you want to spread butter onto your piece of bread. Let your dinner knife take a rest for now. Use your own bread plate now too.

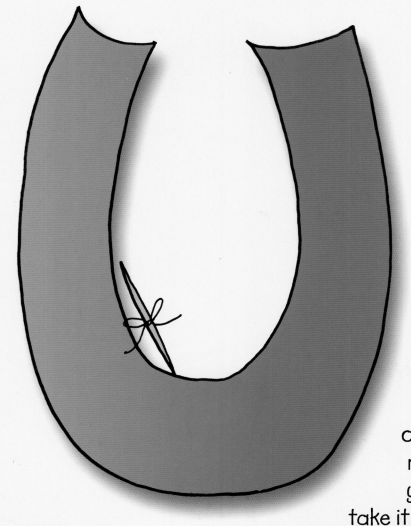

Use a toothpick only when you really need to. As soon as your 'work' is done, take it out of your mouth. It's not a chew toy.

Very curious people should not pick food off of their neighbor's plate. Instead, they should ask for a serving of their own. Your plate of food belongs to YOU; their plate of food belongs to THEM.   If you have something you wish to share, then offer it and pass it around.

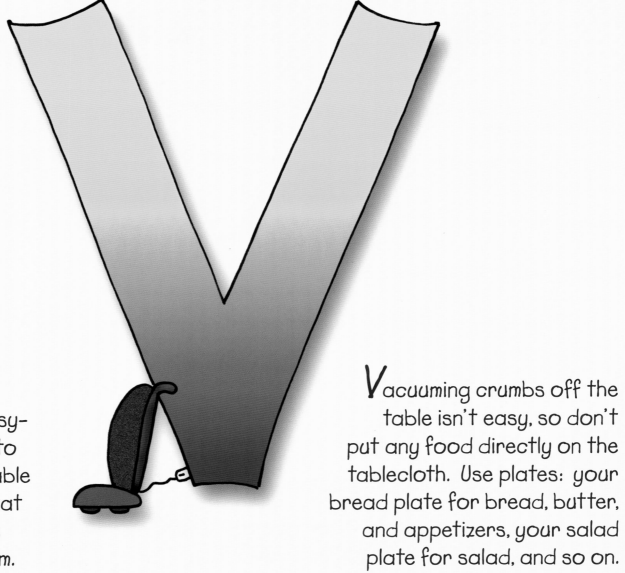

*V*oices that are "easy-medium" are so nice to have at the table. Table talk is not so loud that the next table thinks you're talking to them.

*V*acuuming crumbs off the table isn't easy, so don't put any food directly on the tablecloth. Use plates: your bread plate for bread, butter, and appetizers, your salad plate for salad, and so on.

When a "toast" is being made, everyone raises their glass with cheer ...
EXCEPT for the person being toasted. When you are the one being honored,
you do not lift your glass, or drink from it, until the cheering has finished.

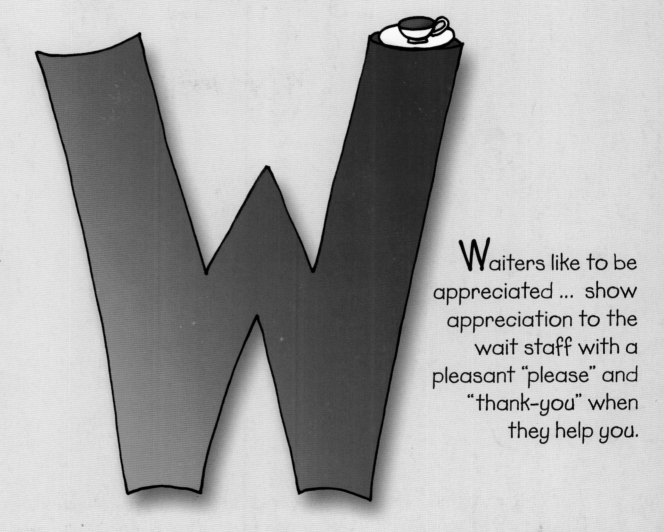

When you don't want a beverage, just say "no, thank you." No need to "flip" your cup or glass upside down, like it's doing a summersault.

Waiters like to be appreciated ... show appreciation to the wait staff with a pleasant "please" and "thank-you" when they help you.

Xylophones make sweet musical sounds.
Telephones used at the dining table create extra noisy and impolite sounds.
Always leave the table if you need to answer or use your cell phone.

"**X**-cuse me!"
Polite conversation never interrupts another person, or starts talking before someone else has finished. Never "cut" another person off with your own ideas. If it's VERY important, say "Excuse me, I am sorry to interrupt, but..."

X-ray eyes can tell if you spit ice back into your glass after drinking. No "backwashing," please.

Yuck! You don't like squash or rhubarb? When something is passed or offered to you and you don't want to have it on your plate, just say a nice "no, thank you."

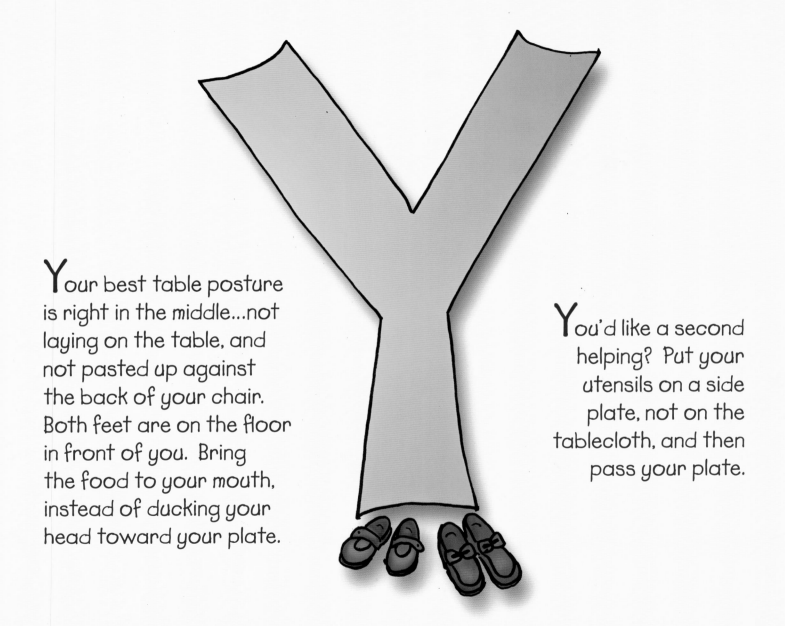

Your best table posture is right in the middle...not laying on the table, and not pasted up against the back of your chair. Both feet are on the floor in front of you. Bring the food to your mouth, instead of ducking your head toward your plate.

You'd like a second helping? Put your utensils on a side plate, not on the tablecloth, and then pass your plate.

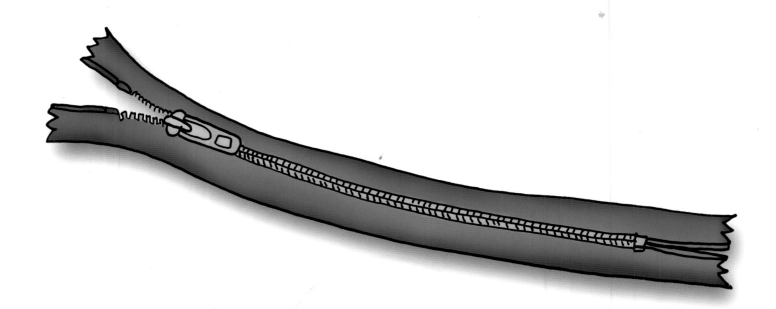

Zip your lips while chewing. No "mouth-open" chomping and stomping, even if you've got good rhythm.

Zoo animals, kittens, puppies, and other pets don't eat at the table with you – unless you are having a special "Pet Party Celebration."

Zero points for licking your fingers – even if they taste SO good. Always use your napkin instead.

"You've Got Manners! " began on a family road trip—a 1,000 mile vacation through Canada the summer of 2002. To pass the time among our three generations in a mini-van, the game of naming and playing with table manner ideas became our car activity. Out of this 'close' time together, and with many dining stops along the way, a book on table tips was born!

Pictured here is the five-member Advisory Board for You've Got Manners Enterprises, who inspired this book, with the author Louise Elerding—referred to as 'Grandy' by her 5 sensational grandkids.
Their quarterly Board meetings are generating ideas and decisions for the future of YGM Enterprises, while seeing all possibilities through the eyes of "kids."

At right, the Advisory Board. In pyramid order, top down and left to right:
Louise
Jason, Alyssa
Amanda, Emily, Tyler

Certificate of Special Achievement

JUST WATCH ME

_____

(Your Name)

I know my Table Tips from A to Z

and

I'VE GOT MANNERS!

Index

...and we've got classes !

MannerSmart   2 classes: 1 hour each
   A basic introduction to Dining Etiquette for ages 11-14 .
   Experience manners from approaching the table, to polite exiting, and the subtle details in-between.

Manners 4 Us   2 classes: 1 hour each
   Simple manner-friendly tips for ages 6-10.
   Learn how dining etiquette at the elementary level can be fun.

Tea party Techniques   2 classes: 30 minutes each
   For boys and girls, ages 3-5 (and their guest bear/doll friends).
   Early manner-awareness, with napkin practice, passing techniques, & social introductions.

For more information on classes, teaching manuals, and curriculum licensing
call 1-800-326-8953 or email: MannersA2Z@aol.com

To locate an Etiquette Consultant in your area, call us for a Certified Image Professional
in the Association of Image Consultants International (AICI).

visit our website: www.youvegotmanners.com

About Louise Elerding

Louise Elerding, AICI, CIP is a Personal Appearance Coach, author, speaker, Image industry trainer, Fashion Feng Shui Facilitator/Trainer, and owner of Professional Image Partners at The Color Studio in Burbank, CA since 1983.

Individuals, businesses, and groups employ Louise to align their inner strengths with their outward appearance - from personal issues to company branding.

Louise is a charter member of the Association of Image Consultants International, AICI, having served as International President 1996-97. She received the esteemed 1999 Award of Excellence from AICI for her contributions to this worldwide industry organization.

In 2001 she was inducted into the International Who's Who of Professional & Business Women's HALL of FAME.

Louise has been quoted in numerous Image books, articles, and publications, among them: Glamour Magazine, L.A. Business Journal, Maximum Style-Rodale Press, the Chicago Tribune, Baltimore Sun, Pacific Sun, One World Live, and CNN.com. Louise also appears on local cable television.

"You've Got Manners! ~ Table Tips from A to Z for Kids of All Ages", along with a small portable spiral-bound companion handbook edition, are her most recent publications. With these books, her "Manners!" teaching curriculum is being used across the country.

BYE for now...

Take your manners with you wherever you go!